JANICE VANCLEAVE'S
CRAZY, KOOKY, AND QUIRKY
SCIENCE EXPERIMENTS

JANICE VANCLEAVE'S
CRAZY, KOOKY, AND QUIRKY
CHEMISTRY
EXPERIMENTS

Illustrations by
Jim Carroll

D0002243

rosen publishing's
rosen
central

New York

This edition published in 2019 by
The Rosen Publishing Group, Inc.
29 East 21st Street
New York, NY 10010

Library of Congress Cataloging-in-Publication Data

Names: VanCleave, Janice Pratt, author.
Title: Janice VanCleave's crazy, kooky, and quirky chemistry experiments / Janice VanCleave.
Description: New York : Rosen Central, 2019 | Series: Janice VanCleave's crazy, kooky, and quirky science experiments | Audience: Grades 5–8. | Includes bibliographical references and index.
Identifiers: LCCN 2017058543| ISBN 9781508180975 (library bound) | ISBN 9781508181026 (pbk.)
Subjects: LCSH: Chemistry—Experiments—Juvenile literature. | Science projects—Juvenile literature.
Classification: LCC QD43 .V3595 2019 | DDC 540.78—dc23
LC record available at https://lccn.loc.gov/2017058543

Manufactured in the United States of America

Experiments first published in *Janice VanCleave's 203 Icy, Freezing, Frosty, Cool, and Wild Experiments* by John Wiley & Sons, Inc. copyright © 1999 Janice VanCleave

CONTENTS

INTRODUCTION

Chemistry is the study of the way materials are put together and their behavior under different conditions. Matter makes up everything in the universe. Chemists study matter to learn what it is made of and how it reacts.

The people who decide to work in the field of chemistry have a variety of careers to choose from. Food chemists study the ingredients in what we eat, doctors study biochemistry and the reactions that take place in the body, and forensic chemists work with crime scene evidence. All of these people have something in common: they are constantly asking questions to learn even more about chemistry.

This book is a collection of science experiments about chemistry. Why are ice pops softer than ice? How does soap clean dirty dishes? Can you test the hardness of water? You will find the answers to these and many other questions by doing the experiments in this book.

HOW TO USE THIS BOOK

You will be rewarded with successful experiments if you read each experiment carefully, follow the steps in order, and do not substitute materials. The following sections are included for all the experiments.

» **PURPOSE:** *The basic goals for the experiment.*

» **MATERIALS:** *A list of supplies you will need.* You will experience less frustration and more fun if you gather all the necessary materials for the experiments before you begin. You lose your train of thought when you have to stop and search for supplies.

» **PROCEDURE:** *Step-by-step instructions on how to perform the experiment.* Follow each step very carefully, never skip steps, and do not add your own. Safety is of the utmost importance, and by reading the experiment before starting, then following the instructions exactly, you can feel confident that no unexpected results will occur. Ask an adult to help you when you are working with anything sharp or hot. If adult supervision is required, it will be noted in the experiment.

» **RESULTS:** *An explanation stating exactly what is expected to happen.* This is an immediate learning tool. If the expected results are achieved, you will know that you did the experiment correctly. If your results are not the same as described in the experiment, carefully read the instructions and start over from the first step.

» **WHY?** *An explanation of why the results were achieved.*

INTRODUCTION

THE SCIENTIFIC METHOD

Scientists identify a problem or observe an event. Then they seek solutions or explanations through research and experimentation. By doing the experiments in this book, you will learn to follow experimental steps and make observations. You will also learn many scientific principles that have to do with chemistry.

In the process, the things you see or learn may lead you to new questions. For example, perhaps you have completed the experiment that studies how you can use the sun to separate salt from water. Now you wonder how humidity might affect the process. That's great! All scientists are curious and ask new questions about what they learn. When you design a new experiment, it is a good idea to follow the scientific method.

1. Ask a question.

2. Do some research about your question. What do you already know?

3. Come up with a hypothesis, or a possible answer to your question.

4. Design an experiment to test your hypothesis. Make sure the experiment is repeatable.

5. Collect the data and make observations.

6. Analyze your results.

7. Reach a conclusion. Did your results support your hypothesis?

Many times the experiment leads to more questions and a new experiment. *Always remember that when devising your own science experiment, have a knowledgeable adult review it with you before trying it out. Ask him or her to supervise it as well.*

EXPANDO

PURPOSE To observe the effects of expanding gas.

MATERIALS empty 2-liter plastic soda bottle
timer
½ cup (125 ml) tap water
1 tablespoon (15 ml) dishwashing liquid
saucer

NOTE: This experiment requires a freezer.

PROCEDURE

1. Place the empty soda bottle in a freezer for two minutes or more.

2. While you are waiting, mix the water and dishwashing liquid together in the saucer.

3. Remove the soda bottle from the freezer and dip its open end in the soapy water.

4. Stand the bottle on a table and observe what happens.

NOTE: If a soap bubble does not form over the mouth, dip the bottle in the soapy water again.

RESULTS A soap bubble forms over the mouth of the bottle.

WHY? As the temperature of molecules decreases, molecular motion decreases and the cohesive force increases, pulling the molecules closer together. Cooling caused the air molecules inside the bottle to move closer together, removed from the freezer, the cold air inside it heated up and the air molecules moved farther apart. Some of the air was forced out of the bottle and pushed on the soap film across the mouth of the bottle, making a soap bubble.

FOAMY

PURPOSE To show how pressure affects dissolved gases.

MATERIALS plastic cereal bowl
16-ounce (480 ml) glass soda bottle
¼ cup (63 ml) tap water
two effervescent antacid tablets

PROCEDURE

1. Set the bowl on a table and stand the soda bottle in it.

2. Pour the water into the bottle.

3. Break the antacid tablets in half.

4. Quickly drop the broken tablets into the bottle of water and immediately cover the mouth of the bottle with the palm of your hand.

5. Observe the contents of the bottle.

6. When it becomes difficult for you to keep your hand over the bottle because of the pressure against your palm, quickly lift your hand and observe what happens to the bottle's contents.

RESULTS The antacid tablets mix with the water, producing bubbles. When the bottle is covered, bubbles are seen in the water and a small amount of foam forms on the surface of the water. Uncovering the bottle produces a bubbly foam that rises within the bottle.

WHY? When the antacid tablets are combined with water, carbon dioxide gas is produced. Covering the opening of the bottle prevents the gas from escaping. As more gas is produced, the pressure inside the bottle increases. Increasing the pressure on any mixture of liquid and gas results in more gas dissolving in the liquid and a reduction in the size of the gas bubbles. Raising your hand allows the excess gas above the water to escape, which quickly reduces the pressure pushing down on the surface of the water. At this lower pressure, many gas bubbles move upward and break through the surface of the liquid. Each bubble rises, rapidly expands, and pushes some of the liquid upward, resulting in the rising foam.

NEW STUFF

PURPOSE To demonstrate a chemical change.

MATERIALS Polident tablet
10-ounce (300 ml) clear plastic drinking glass
tap water
timer

PROCEDURE

1. Observe the appearance of the tablet.

2. Fill the glass about one-half full with water.

3. Drop the tablet into the water and observe the results.

4. Allow the cup to sit for three to five minutes. Then observe the contents of the glass.

RESULTS The tablet is solid when dry. When dropped in the water, it bubbles vigorously. After a few minutes, foamy liquid is seen in the glass.

WHY? The solid tablet combines with liquid water to form a new substance, a gas. A process by which one or more substances are changed into one or more different substances is called a chemical change.

SPEEDY

PURPOSE To determine how temperature affects the speed of a chemical reaction.

MATERIALS

¼ cup (63 ml) cold tap water
two 10-ounce (300 ml) transparent
  plastic drinking glasses
5 to 6 ice cubes
pen
masking tape

timer
spoon
¼ cup (63 ml) warm tap water
2 effervescent antacid tablets

PROCEDURE

1. Pour the cold water into one of the glasses and add the ice cubes. Use the pen and tape to label the glass "Cold."

2. Allow the water and ice to sit for two minutes, stirring periodically.

3. Use the spoon to remove the ice from the water. Discard the ice.

4. Pour the warm water into the other glass. Use the pen and tape to label the glass "Warm."

5. Drop an antacid tablet into each of the glasses at the same time.

6. Don't stir. Observe the tablets to determine which dissolves first.

RESULTS The tablet in the warm water dissolves first.

WHY? In order for a chemical reaction to occur, the molecules of water must combine with the molecules on the surface of the antacid tablet.

14

This combination occurs as the water molecules randomly collide with the molecules on the surface of the tablet. All particles of matter, such as the antacid tablets and the water, have kinetic energy (energy of motion). Kinetic energy increases with temperature. This means the water molecules in the glass of warm water are moving around at a faster speed than those in the glass of cold water. Thus, the rate of collision between warm-water molecules and antacid molecules is greater than that between cold-water molecules and antacid molecules. Thus, an increase in temperature increased the speed of the chemical reaction in this experiment. It might be inferred that this would be true for other chemical reactions.

BROWN BANANA

PURPOSE To determine if vitamin C can inhibit oxidation.

MATERIALS

dinner knife
banana
two saucers
two sheets of printer paper
pen

three vitamin C tables (100 mg
  tablets work well)
cutting board
rolling pin
timer

PROCEDURE

1. Peel the banana, then slice it into eight pieces.

2. Place four slices of banana in each saucer.

3. Set each saucer on a sheet of paper. Label one of the papers "Without Vitamin C" and the other "With Vitamin C."

4. Place the vitamin C tablets on the cutting board and crush them with the rolling pin.

5. Using the dinner knife to scoop up the vitamin C powder, sprinkle the powder over the cut surface of the banana slices in the saucer labeled "With Vitamin C."

6. Every thirty minutes for two hours or more, observe the color of each sample's surface.

RESULTS The untreated banana slices slowly turn brown, but those covered with vitamin C are unchanged.

WHY? Bananas and other fruit, such as apples and pears, discolor when bruised or peeled and exposed to air. This discoloration is caused by changes that occur when the cells are broken. The chemicals released by the damaged cells are oxidized (combined with oxygen), resulting in changes in the fruit. This process is called oxidation. Vitamin C is an antioxidant, a substance that inhibits (decreases or stops) oxidation. Covering the surface of the banana with vitamin C inhibits the discoloration caused by oxidation.

SOAP SCUM

PURPOSE To test for the hardness of water.

MATERIALS

1 tablespoon (15 ml) distilled water
¼ teaspoon (1.2 ml) Epsom salts
small jar with lid
spoon

eyedropper
dishwashing liquid
timer
ruler

PROCEDURE

1. Prepare a sample of hard water by combining the distilled water and Epsom salts in the jar. Stir well.

2. Add one drop of the dishwashing liquid to the jar, then secure the lid.

3. Shake the jar vigorously for fifteen seconds.

4. Observe contents of the jar.

RESULTS Few soap suds form above the water.

WHY? The hardness of water is a measure of the amount of calcium, magnesium, and/or iron salts dissolved in the water. These substances make it difficult for soap to make suds. They combine with the fatty acids (chemicals found in animal and plant fat that are composed of carbon, hydrogen, and oxygen) in soap to form waxy, insoluble (unable to be dissolved) salts. Epsom salts' chemical name is magnesium sulfate. The magnesium in the chemical combines with the fatty acids in the dishwashing liquid to form soap scum instead of soap suds.

Janice VanCleave's Crazy, Kooky, and Quirky Chemistry Experiments

Soap Scum

BUBBLER

PURPOSE To see how carbonates react to acids.

MATERIALS long-handled spoon
raw egg
1 quart (1 liter) widemouthed jar
white vinegar

CAUTION: *Wash your hands after handling raw eggs. They can contain harmful bacteria.*

PROCEDURE

1. Use the spoon to place the egg in the jar, being careful not to crack the egg.

2. Fill the jar with vinegar.

3. Observe the appearance of the eggshell immediately and then periodically for the next two days.

RESULTS Bubbles start forming immediately on the surface of the eggshell and increase in number over time. After about two days, the shell is no longer present, and a membrane, which is a thin, filmlike outer layer around the egg, holds the egg together.

WHY? Chemicals containing combinations of carbon and oxygen with some other element, such as calcium, barium, or manganese, are called carbonates. The main ingredient of the eggshell is calcium carbonate. Vinegar is a mixture of water and an acid (a type of chemical that produces hydrogen ions—charged particles—when dissolved in water).

When calcium carbonate combines with an acid, such as vinegar, new substances are produced, including carbon dioxide gas. The bubbles seen rising in the jar are carbon dioxide gas.

CLUMPED

PURPOSE To demonstrate the effect of calcium ions on milk coagulation.

MATERIALS masking tape
marking pen
two 10-ounce (300 ml) clear plastic drinking glasses
½ cup (125 ml) skim milk in measuring cup
½ teaspoon (2.5 ml) Epsom salts
two spoons
2 teaspoons (10 ml) vinegar

PROCEDURE

1. Use the tape and pen to label the glasses A and B.

2. Pour ¼ cup (63 ml) of milk into each glass.

3. Add the Epsom salts to glass A and stir until it dissolves in the milk.

4. Using a separate spoon for each glass, dip a spoonful of milk out of each glass and compare their appearances.

5. Add 1 teaspoon (5 ml) of vinegar to both glasses.

6. Using the same spoons used in step 4 for each glass, stir to mix the vinegar and milk. Again, dip and compare the spoonfuls of milk.

RESULTS The milk in glass B contains clumps. The milk in glass A does not have clumps.

WHY? Vinegar, an acid, causes milk to coagulate (clump), such as happened in glass B. But the coagulation of milk can only happen if calcium ions (charged particles) are present in the milk. The milk in glass A did not coagulate because the Epsom salts reacted with the calcium ions to produce an insoluble calcium compound. The calcium ions were no longer present in the milk and thus could not cause coagulation.

A New Look

PURPOSE To observe a physical change.

MATERIALS 4-inch (10 cm) circle of black construction paper
saucer
1 tablespoon (15 ml) table sugar
magnifying lens
¼ cup (63 ml) tap water

PROCEDURE

1. Place the black paper circle in the saucer.

2. Sprinkle a few crystals of sugar on the paper, and use the magnifying lens to observe the sugar crystals.

3. Put all of the sugar in the cup of water. Stir until no sugar crystals are visible with your naked eye.

4. Dip out a spoonful of the liquid, and use the magnifying lens to look for sugar crystals in the water.

RESULTS When dry, the sugar crystals look like tiny white cubes. When the sugar crystals are mixed with the water, they are not visible.

WHY? The sugar crystals dissolve in the water. Dissolving is the process by which a solute (a material that dissolves) breaks up and thoroughly mixes with a solvent (a material in which a solute dissolves). Dissolving is a physical change that produces a solution (a combination of a solute and a solvent). A physical change is one in which the appearance of matter changes, but its properties and makeup remain unchanged. The sugar breaks into particles not visible even with the magnifying lens, but they are still sugar.

INK

PURPOSE To produce a mixture.

MATERIALS red, blue, and yellow food coloring
4-inch (10 cm) square of waxed paper
toothpick
printer paper

PROCEDURE

1. Place one drop of each food coloring in the center of the waxed paper.

2. With the toothpick, stir the colors together. This will be your ink.

3. Using the toothpick, write your name on the printer paper with the ink.

NOTE: Keep the ink for the next experiment.

RESULTS A dark ink mixture is formed.

WHY? The combination of the food colors is a mixture. A mixture is made of two or more substances that are physically combined. A physical combination is one in which the parts retain their separate properties and can be separated. (To separate the colors, see the next experiment.)

SEPARATED

PURPOSE To separate the parts of a mixture.

MATERIALS 3.25-inch (8.25 cm) basket-type coffee filter
round toothpick
ink from the experiment "Ink"
timer
cup of tap water

PROCEDURE

1. Stand the coffee filter upside down on a table.

2. Wet the end of the toothpick in the ink.

3. Touch the wet end of the toothpick to the center of the coffee filter to make a small dot of color.

4. Repeat steps 2 and 3 to make eight to ten small colored dots near the center of the coffee filter.

5. Allow the coffee filter to stand undisturbed until the ink on the paper dries. This should take two to three minutes.

6. Wet the tip of one finger in the water, then touch the center of the coffee filter.

7. Repeat step 6 twice, touching a different part of the paper so that all of the colored dots are wet by the water.

8. Without disturbing the paper, observe the colors on the paper periodically for twenty to thirty minutes.

RESULTS The ink separates into three different colors: yellow, red, and blue.

WHY? The method of separating the ink mixture into its parts is called chromatography. This method of separating is based on different factors, one of which is adhesive force. The color in the ink that has the least attraction to the paper moves fastest and farthest across the paper. The other colors move at slower speeds and shorter distances, and the one with the greatest attraction to the paper moves the slowest and the least. In this experiment, the blue color moved fastest and farthest, followed by yellow, then red.

wet fingertip

THE SAME

PURPOSE To make a homogenous mixture.

MATERIALS

spoon
drinking glass
dishwashing liquid
tap water

paper towel
distilled water
1 teaspoon (5 ml) sugar
drinking straw

PROCEDURE

NOTE: Never taste anything in a laboratory setting unless you are sure that there are no harmful chemicals or materials and that all containers are properly cleaned. This experiment is safe since only sugar and water are used.

1. Prepare the materials by washing the spoon and glass in soapy water.

2. Rinse the spoon and glass in clear water, and dry them with the paper towel.

3. Fill the cleaned glass half full with distilled water.

4. Add the sugar to the distilled water.

5. Stir until no sugar particles can be seen.

6. Stand a clean straw in the glass containing the sugar-water mixture.

7. Hold your finger on the top of the straw as you raise the straw out of the glass. (The sugar-water mixture stays in the straw.) Place the bottom of the straw on your tongue. Taste the liquid, and make a mental note of its sweetness.

Janice VanCleave's Crazy, Kooky, and Quirky Chemistry Experiments

8. Use the straw to taste samples from the bottom, middle, and top of the sugar-water mixture.

9. Compare the taste of the three samples.

RESULTS All three samples have the same sweet taste.

WHY? Sugar and water form a special mixture called a solution. Solutions are produced by combining a solute with a solvent. The solute (sugar) dissolves in the solvent (water). The molecules in the crystals of sugar separate and move between the molecules of water. The sugar-water solution is homogeneous, meaning the solution is the same throughout. Samples of equal volume taken from the solution would contain the same number of sugar molecules and water molecules regardless of where the samples were taken.

The Same

SUN TEA

PURPOSE To determine how temperature affects how quickly a solute dissolves.

MATERIALS two 1-quart (1 liter) jars with lids
cold tap water
four tea bags
timer

PROCEDURE

1. Fill the jars with water.

2. Add two tea bags to each of the jars. Secure the lids on both jars.

3. At or near noon on a sunny day, set one jar outside in direct sunlight.

4. Set the remaining jar in the refrigerator.

5. Every thirty minutes for two hours, compare the color of the liquid in each jar.

RESULTS The liquid in the jar outside became dark more quickly than did the liquid in the jar in the refrigerator.

WHY? Heat from the sun caused an increase in the temperature of the water in the jar that you put outdoors. Generally, a solute dissolves more quickly in a warm solvent than in a cold one. So the solute (the substance in the tea leaves) dissolved more quickly in the water warmed by the sun, causing the water to become dark faster.

Sun Tea

PULLERS

PURPOSE To demonstrate hydration.

MATERIALS 10-ounce (300 ml) transparent plastic drinking glass
cold tap water
small piece of chocolate candy

PROCEDURE

1. Fill the glass about three-fourths full with water.

2. Put the candy into the water.

3. Observe the area where the water touches the candy.

RESULTS Dark streams of material move away from the candy's surface.

WHY? When the candy (solute) is added to the water (solvent), it dissolves to form a solution. The dissolving of the candy occurs because water molecules randomly move about, colliding with the surface of the candy. While the cohesive force of the candy molecules holds them together, the adhesive force between the water molecules and candy molecules is great enough to pull the candy molecules off the candy's surface. Because of the attraction of the water molecules to the candy molecules, each of the freed candy molecules becomes completely surrounded by water molecules. This process by which water molecules surround a solute molecule is called hydration. The candy molecules that leave the candy along with their cluster of water molecules are said to be hydrated (surrounded by water molecules). As the surface layer of candy molecules is hydrated, the next layer is exposed to the water.

PLUMP

PURPOSE To demonstrate rehydration.

MATERIALS twenty raisins

two 10-ounce (300 ml) clear plastic drinking glasses

tap water

PROCEDURE

1. Place ten raisins in each glass.

2. Fill one of the glasses with water. Observe the appearance of the raisins in each glass.

3. Allow the glasses to sit undisturbed overnight. During this time, observe the raisins in each glass as often as possible. Compare the size and shape of the raisins in each glass.

RESULTS All the raisins look wrinkled at the start of the experiment. Over time, the appearance of the raisins in the glass without water does not change. But the raisins covered with water increase in size and their shape is more rounded.

WHY? Raisins are made by dehydrating (removing water from) grapes. Before the dehydration process, grapes are round. Like all plants, grapes are made up of cells with rather stiff cell walls. When water is removed from the cells, the walls are generally not changed, but the cells collapse without the water to fill them. When the dehydrated fruit is placed in water, the cells fill with water and resume their original shape. Reconstitution is the process of rehydrating (restoring water to) dried food, which means the cells of the food are returned to their original hydrated form. Rehydration doesn't return food to its exact original shape or taste.

Plump

SWOLLEN

PURPOSE To demonstrate absorption.

MATERIALS two 10-ounce clear plastic drinking glasses
two identical gummy candies
timer

PROCEDURE

1. Fill one of the glasses about three-fourths full with water.

2. Place a gummy candy in each glass.

3. Place the glasses where they will be undisturbed, but in view.

4. Observe the candy every hour for six or more hours.

NOTE: After the experiment is completed, discard the candy.

RESULTS The candy in the glass without water remains unchanged, but the candy in the water swells.

WHY? The process by which one substance takes in another, such as a sponge soaking up water, or as in this experiment, candy soaking up water, is called absorption. An increase in the volume of a substance is a good indication of absorption. Solids and liquids may also absorb gases. The candy in the glass without water did not noticeably change in size, so it can be assumed that either it did not absorb air, or the amount absorbed was not enough to make a visual difference in size.

Swollen

CLEANSING POWER

PURPOSE To determine the cleansing effect of dishwashing liquid.

MATERIALS

four clear drinking glasses
tap water
masking tape
marking pen

three 1-teaspoon (5 ml) measuring spoons
cooking oil
dishwashing
liquid timer

PROCEDURE

1. Fill each glass half full with water.

2. Use the masking tape and marking pen to number the glasses 1 through 4.

3. Use one of the spoons to add 1 teaspoon (5 ml) of cooking oil to glasses 2 and 4. Leave the spoon in glass 2.

4. Using a second spoon, add 1 teaspoon (5 ml) of dishwashing liquid to glasses 3 and 4. Leave the spoon in glass 4.

5. Place the third spoon in glass 3.

6. Stir the contents of glasses 2, 3, and 4 ten turns each.

7. Allow the glasses to stand undisturbed for 5 minutes.

8. Observe the appearance of the contents of each glass.

RESULTS The contents of glasses 1 and 3 are clear. The contents of glass 2 have circles of oil floating on the surface, and those of glass 4 look cloudy.

WHY? Glass 1 shows the appearance of water, which is clear. Glass 2 shows the appearance of a mixture of water and oil. The oil does not dissolve in the water, and soon after the stirring stops, the oil separates, forming a layer on top of the water. Glasses 3 and 4 contain detergent from the dishwashing liquid. Detergent molecules are long and have one end that attracts water and another end that attracts oil. Stirring the liquid in glass 4 breaks the oil into tiny droplets. Detergent molecules surround and attach to each drop of oil. The outside of the detergent molecule attaches to water drops. The oil remains as tiny drops suspended throughout the water but separated from it by a protective coat of detergent molecules. This allows oily dirt to be removed from dishes and dissolved in the dishwater containing detergent. The dissolved oil clouds the water in glass 4. Because there is no oil in glass 3, the water remains clear.

DETERGENT MOLECULE

SUN DRIED

PURPOSE To use the sun to separate salt from salty water.

MATERIALS

cookie sheet

two sheets of black construction paper

2 tablespoons (30 ml) table salt

1 cup (250 ml)

tap water

spoon

PROCEDURE

1. Cover the bottom of the cookie sheet with the black paper.

2. Add the salt to the water in the cup and stir. Most, but usually not all, of the salt will dissolve.

3. Pour the salty water over the paper. Try not to pour any undissolved salt onto the paper. Allow the undissolved salt to remain in the cup.

4. Place the cookie sheet in a sunny place where it will not be disturbed for several days. This can be by a window or outdoors if the weather is warm and dry.

5. Observe the paper daily until it is dry.

RESULTS A thin layer of white crystals forms on the paper. A few small, white, cubic crystals form after several days.

WHY? As the sun heats the salty water, the water evaporates and dry salt is left on the paper. This experiment is similar to a method used by some salt companies to produce salt by the evaporation of water from seawater.

Sun Dried

ICY

PURPOSE To determine why ice pops are softer than ice.

MATERIALS

1-quart (1 liter) jar
tap water
2-quart (2 liter) pitcher
0.15-ounce (4.3 g) package of unsweetened
   flavored powdered drink mix
1½ cups (375 ml) granulated sugar

spoon
two 3-ounce (90 ml) paper cups
plate
two craft sticks
freezer

PROCEDURE

1. Pour 1 quart (1 liter) of water into the pitcher. Add the drink mix and the sugar to the water and stir.

2. Place the paper cups on the plate.

3. Fill one of the cups with tap water and the other cup with the drink.

4. Stand a craft stick in each cup.

5. Set the plate in the freezer.

6. The next day, remove the plate from the freezer. Peel the paper cup away from the frozen liquids.

7. Holding the craft sticks, carefully try to bite into the ice pop (the frozen drink) and the ice (the frozen water).

NOTE: Use the remaining drink and twelve cups and sticks to prepare extra ice pops to eat later or share with friends.

RESULTS The liquid drink and water both changed to solids, but the ice pop is not as firm as the ice. It is easier to bite into the ice pop than the ice.

WHY? The water molecules in each liquid combine to form ice crystals that join together in a solid block. In the ice pop, the ice crystals are separated in some places by sugar molecules and other ingredients in the drink mix, forming smaller ice crystals. These smaller ice crystals make the ice pops easier to eat than the frozen water, which has larger ice crystals.

THINNER

PURPOSE To compare the viscosity of different liquids.

MATERIALS thick book
cookie sheet
four eyedroppers
four liquids: water, hand cream, baby oil, baby lotion
helper

PROCEDURE

1. Use the book to raise one end of the cookie sheet.

2. Fill each eyedropper with a different liquid.

3. With the assistance of a helper, place one drop of each liquid on the raised end of the cookie sheet at the same time.

4. Observe and compare how long it takes each of the liquids to roll down the cookie sheet. This measure is called the liquids' flow rate.

RESULTS The flow rates will depend on the liquids used. In the author's test, the water moved the fastest, followed by the oil, then the lotion. The hand cream barely moved at all.

WHY? Viscosity is a measure of how fast a liquid flows. The least viscous liquid, or the one with the least viscosity, will have the fastest flow rate.

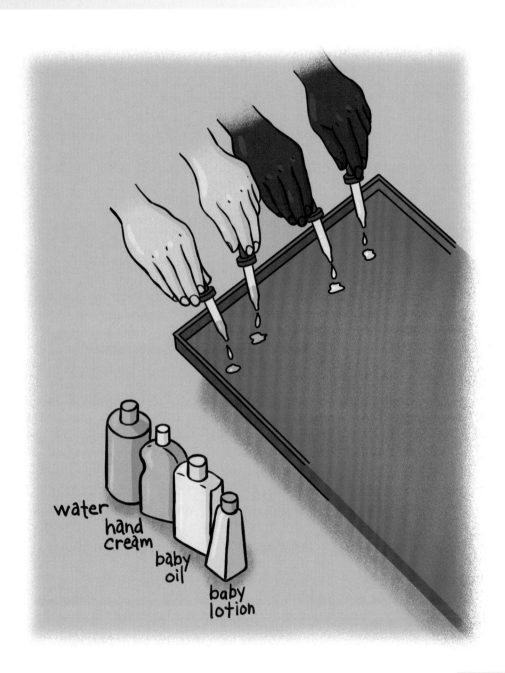

water
hand
cream
baby
oil
baby
lotion

FLOW RATE

PURPOSE To make and use a viscometer.

MATERIALS

scissors
clear plastic dish
detergent bottle with a pull top
marking pen
ruler
modeling clay

glass jar with a mouth slightly smaller than
   the upper part of the detergent bottle
water
timer
adult helper

PROCEDURE

1. Have an adult cut off the bottom of the detergent bottle.

2. Holding the bottle upside down, use the marking pen to make two short straight lines. Make the first line about 1 inch (2.5 cm) from the cutoff edge and the second line 4 inches (10 cm) from the first line.

3. Label the first line "Start" and the second line "Stop." Close the pull top.

4. Place a ring of clay around the top edge of the jar's mouth, then stand the bottle upside down on the jar. Mold the clay ring so that the bottle stands upright, but do not secure the bottle with the clay.

5. Fill the bottle with cold tap water to about ½ inch (1.3 cm) above the start line.

6. Lift the bottle and pull the top open, then immediately set the bottle back on the jar.

7. When the water level reaches the start line, time how long it takes the water level to reach the stop line.

RESULTS The flow rate varies depending on the bottle used. The author's flow rate for cold water was 39.3 seconds.

WHY? A viscometer is an instrument that measures a liquid's viscosity. The amount of time it takes a liquid to flow out of a container depends on its viscosity. The viscometer can be used to measure flow rates of other liquids. Liquids with a low viscosity will flow faster than liquids with a high viscosity.

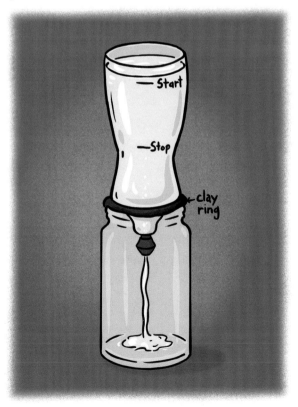

ACID TESTING

PURPOSE To use litmus to test for the presence of an acid.

MATERIALS 1 teaspoon (5 ml) white vinegar

saucer

two strips of litmus paper: one red, one blue

PROCEDURE

1. Put the vinegar in the saucer.

2. Dip one end of the red litmus paper in the vinegar.

3. Observe any change in color of the paper.

4. Repeat steps 2 and 3, using the blue litmus.

RESULTS The blue litmus turns red, but the red litmus does not change color (except perhaps to become redder).

WHY? Litmus is a substance obtained from lichen, a plantlike organism. Litmus acts as a chemical indicator, which means it can be used to determine the presence of an acid or a base. Acids turn blue litmus red, but do not change the color of red litmus. Bases (a type of chemical that produces hydroxide ions) turn red litmus blue, but do not change the color of blue litmus. Since the red litmus did not change color in the vinegar but the blue litmus turned red, vinegar must be an acid.

Acid Testing

BASE TESTING

PURPOSE To use litmus to test for the presence of a base.

MATERIALS spoon
½ teaspoon (2.5 ml) baking soda
1 teaspoon (5 ml) tap water
saucer
two strips of litmus paper: one blue, one red

PROCEDURE

1. Use the spoon to mix the baking soda and water together in the saucer.

2. Dip one end of the blue litmus paper in the liquid.

3. Observe any change in color of the paper.

4. Repeat steps 2 and 3, using the red litmus.

RESULTS The blue litmus does not change color (except perhaps to become bluer), but the red litmus turns blue.

WHY? Bases are a type of chemical that turn red litmus blue but have no effect on the color of blue litmus. Since the red litmus turned blue in the baking-soda-and-water mixture but the blue litmus did not change color, baking soda must be a base.

EDIBLE ACID

PURPOSE To identify an edible acid.

MATERIALS saucer
strip of blue litmus paper
½ lemon

PROCEDURE

1. Lay the litmus paper in the saucer.

2. Squeeze a drop of lemon juice on one end of the paper.

3. Observe any change in the color of the litmus paper.

RESULTS The blue litmus turns red.

WHY? Since blue litmus turns red in an acid, lemon juice must be an acid. Lemon juice is an edible acid used in making foods, including lemonade and lemon pie.

blue
litmus

GLOSSARY

ABSORPTION The process by which one substance takes in another.

ACID A type of chemical that produces hydrogen ions—charged particles—when dissolved in water.

ANTIOXIDANT A substance that decreases or stops oxidation.

BASE A type of chemical that produces hydroxide ions.

CARBONATE A chemical that contains a combination of carbon and oxygen with some other element.

CHEMICAL CHANGE A process by which one or more substances are changed into one or more different substances.

COAGULATE To clump.

DEHYDRATE To remove water from.

DISSOLVE The process by which a solute breaks up and thoroughly mixes with a solvent.

FATTY ACID A chemical found in animal and plant fat that is composed of carbon, hydrogen, and oxygen.

HOMOGENOUS The same throughout.

HYDRATED Surrounded by water molecules.

INSOLUBLE Not able to be dissolved.

KINETIC ENERGY The energy of motion.

OXIDIZATION Any chemical reaction in which a substance combines with oxygen.

PHYSICAL CHANGE A process by which the appearance of matter changes but its properties and makeup remain unchanged.

RECONSTITUTION The process of restoring water to dried food.

REHYDRATE To restore water to.

SOLUTE A material that dissolves.

SOLUTION A combination of a solute and a solvent.

SOLVENT A material in which a solute dissolves.

FOR MORE INFORMATION

American Association for the Advancement of Science (AAAS)
1200 New York Avenue NW
Washington, DC 20005
(202) 326-6400
Website: http://www.aaas.org
The AAAS has been promoting the advancement of science for over 150 years. Take part in Family Science Days, learn about the latest discoveries through their daily Science Update, or see their choices for the best science books for kids.

American Chemical Society (ACS)
1155 Sixteenth Street NW
Washington, DC 20036
(800) 333-9511
Website: http://www.acs.org
The American Chemical Society has free educational resources, including experiments and games in their Adventures in Chemistry program, high school chemistry clubs, the Chemistry Olympiad competition for students, and Project SEED summer research programs. They educate the public during National Chemistry Week.

Chemical Institute of Canada
222 Queen Street, Suite 400
Ottawa, ON K1P 5V9
Canada
(888) 542-2242
Website: http://www.cheminst.ca
The Chemical Institute of Canada provides information about science fairs, scholarships, and the Canadian Chemistry Contest.

National Science Foundation (NSF)
  4201 Wilson Boulevard
  Arlington, VA 22230
  (703) 292-5111
  Website: http://www.nsf.gov
  The NSF is dedicated to science, engineering, and education. Learn how to be a Citizen Scientist, read about the latest scientific discoveries, and find out about the newest innovations in technology.

Society for Science and the Public
  Student Science
  1719 N Street NW
  Washington, DC 20036
  (800) 552-4412
  Website: http://student.societyforscience.org
  The Society for Science and the Public presents many science resources, such as science news for students, the latest updates on the Intel Science Talent Search and the Intel International Science and Engineering Fair, and information about cool jobs and doing science.

FOR FURTHER READING

Biskup, Agnieszka. *Super Cool Chemical Reaction Activities with Max Axiom* (Max Axiom Science and Engineering Activities). North Mankato, MN: Capstone Press, 2015.

Buczynski, Sandy. *Designing a Winning Science Fair Project* (Information Explorer Junior). Ann Arbor, MI: Cherry Lake Publishing, 2014.

Cobb, Vicki. *Science Experiments You Can Eat.* New York, NY: Harper, 2016.

Gardner, Jane P. *Chemistry*. Broomall, PA: Mason Crest, 2017.

Heinecke, Liz Lee. *Outdoor Science Lab for Kids: 52 Family-Friendly Experiments for the Yard, Garden, Playground, and Park.* Beverly, MA: Quarry Books, 2016.

Henneberg, Susan. *Creating Science Fair Projects with Cool New Digital Tools* (Way Beyond PowerPoint: Making 21st Century Presentations). New York, NY: Rosen Central, 2014.

Mercer, Bobby. *Junk Drawer Chemistry: 50 Awesome Experiments that Don't Cost a Thing*. Chicago, IL: Chicago Review Press, 2015.

Miller, Rachel. *The 101 Coolest Simple Science Experiments: Awesome Things to Do with Your Parents, Babysitters, and Other Adults*. Salem, MA: Page Street Publishing Co., 2016.

Navarro, Paula. *Incredible Experiments with Chemical Reactions and Mixtures* (Magic Science). Hauppague, NY: Barron's Educational Series, 2014.

O'Quinn, Amy M. Marie *Curie for Kids: Her Life and Scientific*

Discoveries with 21 Activities and Experiments. Chicago, IL: Chicago Review Press, 2017.

Rompella, Natalie. *Experiments in Material and Matter with Toys and Everyday Stuff* (First Facts: Fun Science). North Mankato, MN: Capstone Press, 2016.

Ruff Ruffman's *44 Favorite Science Activities* (Fetch! with Ruff Ruffman). Somerville, MA: Candlewick Press, 2015.

Thomas, Isabel. *Experiments with Materials* (Read and Experiment). Chicago, IL: Heinemann Raintree, 2016.

Weakland, Mark. *Kaboom! Wile E. Coyote Experiments with Chemical Reactions*. North Mankato, MN: Capstone Press, 2017.

INDEX

A
absorption, 38
acid, 18–22, 50, 54
adhesive force, 29, 34
adult supervision, 5, 7, 48
air molecules, 8–9
antioxidant, 17

B
barium, 20
bases, 50, 52

C
calcium, 18, 20, 22–23
calcium carbonate, 20–21
calcium ion, 22–23
carbon, 10, 18
carbonates, 20–21
carbon dioxide, 10, 21
cell walls, 36
chemical change, 12
chemical indicator, 50
chemical reaction, 14–15
chemistry definition, 4
chromatography, 29
coagulation, 22–23
cohesive force, 8, 34
crystals, 24, 31, 42, 45

D
dehydration, 36
detergent, 41
dissolving, 10, 14, 18, 20, 22, 24, 31, 32, 40, 41–42
doctors, 4

E
Epsom salts, 18, 22–23
evaporation, 42

F
fatty acids, 18
food chemists, 4
forensic chemists, 4

G
gas, 8, 10–11, 12, 20–21, 38

H
homogeneous, 31
hydration, 34, 36
hydrogen, 18, 20
hypothesis, 7

I
insolubility, 18, 23
ions, 20, 22–23, 50

iron salts, 18

K
kinetic energy, 15

L
lichen, 50
litmus, 50, 52, 54

M
magnesium, 18
manganese, 20
matter, 4, 15, 24
membrane, 20
mixture, 11, 20, 26, 28–31, 41, 52
molecular motion, 8
molecules, 8–9, 14–15, 31, 34,
    41, 45

O
oil, 41, 46
oxidation, 16–17
oxygen, 17–18, 20

P
physical combination, 24, 26

R
reconstitution, 36

S
safety, 5
scientific method, 6–7
soap, 4, 8–9, 18, 30
solids, 38, 45
solute, 24, 31–32, 34
solutions, 6, 24, 31, 34
solvent, 24, 31–32, 34

V
viscometer, 48–49
viscosity, 46, 49
vitamin C, 16–17
volume, 31, 38